FIFTY WAYS YOU CAN FEED A HUNGRY WORLD

Fifty Ways You Can Feed a Hungry World

TONY CAMPOLO & GORDON AESCHLIMAN

KINGSWAY PUBLICATIONS

EASTBOURNE

Biblical quotations are from the
New International Version © 1973, 1978, 1984
by the International Bible Society.

Cover design by
Fish Graphics Design Consultancy

ISBN 0 85476 297 3

Printed in Great Britain for
KINGSWAY PUBLICATIONS LTD
Lottbridge Drove, Eastbourne, E. Sussex BN23 6NT by
Clays Ltd, St. Ives plc
Typeset by J&L Composition Ltd, Filey, North Yorkshire

Our special thanks to Chuck Shelton for his creative assistance in the development of these fifty ideas.

Also to Dave Cave for his valuable input into the British edition of this book.

Contents

Introduction

Hunger Is As Big As Poverty

Fortunately, few Christians carry the stereotype that hungry people are those who are too lazy to work. What does cause hunger, however, is not always clear to us.

Hunger does not stand in isolation. It is not the one-time result of lack of rain (drought) or crop failure (famine). Rather, it is linked to a web of factors that include war, illiteracy, disease, contaminated water, oppressive governments, drug abuse, environmental destruction, poor housing, lack of education, and crime—to name just a few.

Sadly, hunger's biggest statistic relates to defenceless children. Jeff Sellers in *World Vision* magazine summarises their plight:

- Children have always been victims of war, but in the past decade an increasing number of children, some as young as eight, have been used to fight as soldiers in many conflicts.

- Drugs and alcohol are affecting children in rural and suburban areas as well as in the world's cities. Crack is the leading cause of illness among infants, children and adolescents living in US cities, according to New York City Health Commissioner Steve Joseph.

- Millions of children are deprived of an education because they must work to help support their families. They are often exploited and forced to work in hazardous conditions for low wages. In some countries, children are preferred as workers

7

over unskilled adults because adults are harder to intimidate and might demand better conditions.

- As many as 100 million children may be living on urban streets around the world. Most of these children have no family. Some have been abandoned; others have run away from home because they are mistreated or ignored.

- Six preventable diseases—measles, whooping cough, diptheria, tuberculosis, polio and tetanus—are responsible for the deaths of millions of children every year. Many more die from dehydration (easily prevented with sugar and water).

- In some countries, only a fraction of the children receive even a few years of education. Girls and disabled children are even less likely to receive an education, crippling their chances to grow into self-sufficient adults.

Caring for 'the least of these' has never been more pressing and demanding than today. And children who suffer the lack of good nutrition today will become dependent on others' care during their entire adult lives because of brain damage resulting from the absence of essential nutrients during critical developmental stages.

More than 40,000 human beings die every day from hunger-related problems. Africa right now is the cradle of desperation where as many as twenty million risk starvation between Ethiopia, Sudan, Mozambique and Angola. But poverty can also be found in the West. More than thirty-two million Americans live below the government's poverty line—forty per cent of them children—and as many as four million Americans live on the streets. A few more statistics paint the picture of America's poverty:

In 1989, substance-abusing mothers gave birth to 375,000 babies; 470,000 were born to single, unemployed teenage mothers. Twenty-five per cent of all pregnant women receive no pre-natal care, while the United States ranks eighteenth internationally in infant mortality. Twenty-five per cent of high school students drop out before they receive their diploma and seventy-five per cent are unable to write a letter seeking employment. (Gordon Aeschliman, *Global Trends* (InterVarsity Press: Illinois, USA, 1990)

Clearly, the hungry world will require a complete and intelligent response from Christians. We are fortunate that God has given us not only hearts of compassion but also heads that can think and skills that can engage the most difficult of hunger's challenges.

This book, *Fifty Ways You Can Feed a Hungry World*, is intentionally written to help those who are already motivated to make a difference. Our scope is broad in that we call for involvement on the whole continuum of poverty; our suggestions are mostly simple, because we don't believe God reserves the privilege of feeding the hungry for the elite; and our approach is upbeat because we do not see this massive task as our duty—rather, it is a labour of love. We feel it is an honour to minister back to Jesus as we take little steps of faith, hope and love.

We do hope you will join us.

Section 1

LIFESTYLE

In this section on lifestyle, the basic approach for all of us is to connect all of our resources to the hungry world—resources such as time, our minds, money, food and cars. We all have much more than we realise and, without too much effort, could free some of God's blessings to be used for the sake of others.

It's possible to become overwhelmed by the vastness of the hungry world and, in fact, to become mired in guilt for having so much. But we must take heart: God has not asked us to be responsible for the problem of world hunger. Rather, God has offered us the privilege of participating in the lives of others out of the wealth he has put in our care.

Every little bit we do makes a difference. Every act of caring is a dignified and worthwhile response to the hungry world. Some are blessed with great organisational skills or engineering gifts—these Christians will minister to the hungry at structural levels across national boundaries, in governmental programmes and through co-ordination of international projects. Most of us, however, have been blessed with a compassionate spirit and the ability to perform simple acts of love that, together, will make a wonderful difference.

Jesus said that to give a needy person a cup of water, some clothes or a little food is to minister directly to Jesus—so profound an impact from such simple giving! And the Lord loves a gracious giver. The lifestyle ideas that follow are not meant to inflict guilt on us for having so much; on the contrary, they are ideas for Christians whose hearts have been set free to reach out in joy, to give to others as a 'thank offering' for all that God has given us.

Enjoy . . .

1

Pass the Crisps

Very few of us don't like to eat. And nothing spoils our appetite more than the unexpected image of a hungry child on the TV screen just as our teeth are about to crunch into the third mouthful of salt and vinegar crisps. How can we enjoy food while others starve?

The fact that we're bothered by that TV image is simply a measure of compassion—we really do care. God created us to require food, so obviously we can't stop eating. But we can do something. We can plan our eating in a way that adequately meets our needs, and then we can put the money we would have spent unnecessarily on ourselves towards providing for those who don't have food.

Take Stock

The best way to begin is simply to understand your eating habits. Spend the next week listing your consumption. Notice what you like to eat most, when you eat and how much you spend on food. Notice when you eat out and how much that costs you. Once you're armed with the information, you need to take action.

Make Your Move

You'll be most nervous about cutting back on your eating when you think you're going to miss out on your favourite foods. Dealing with this dilemma, however, is actually quite easy: Plan your party. Continue to indulge (with delight) in your favourite beverage and snack, but cut out the rest of your excessive eating as your end of the bargain. The leftover money then goes to people who do not have enough.

Try that idea and see if it works for you. Here are some other possibilities:

- Fast once a week—perhaps two meals or a whole day. Calculate the money saved and give it away. Spend the 'fast' time learning more about the hungry world or praying for people in need.

- Make a visit to a restaurant a rare and special treat when you can enjoy the provision of God. Match what you might have spent on a meal and send that amount to a relief and development ministry.

- Link up with a couple of friends once a week for a salad or hamburger. Throw an equivalent amount of money into a jar, and then once a month send that total to your local Salvation Army centre or a similar ministry. A little bit of money really does go far in fighting poverty. The cost of just one dinner among a few friends, say £15, could provide food, medical care and education to a child in Angola for an entire month.

2

Looking Good

Initially it was no problem for Adam and Eve. But after they took a bite of the apple, they had to cover their birthday suits with clothes. Their fig-leaf attempt did not look too good to God's designer eyes, so he took off half a day to sew them the first-ever 'label' clothes—'Holy Threads'.

It's important to us to be accepted by others. We cannot feel guilty about that: God made us to need each other. Advertising, however, has turned that need into an annual multi-million-pound opportunity, and consequently most of us spend much more on our drive to look good than we really need to. We can make some changes without looking like slobs—and yes, we can keep our friends.

Take Stock

If we're going to take action, we need to know what we have. Plan ahead for a period of time that is adequate to attack your wardrobe. Clear out everything. Make piles according to category, including shoes, dressing gowns, socks, jackets, dresses and blouses. You're ready for action.

Make Your Move

The first job is to identify those clothes that have a significantly high scruff factor. If you know you're not going to wear them,

15

abandon them. Don't burden OXFAM with your rubbish: Turn it into useful rags, sewing scraps or dressing-up clothes for school plays.

Now comes the challenge: What do you seriously not need? Be firm with yourself (we all have our different standards), and set aside everything that you consider excessive. Perhaps you will want a friend to help. Think through your living routine to understand how many changes you require within each category. Neatly pack the piles of extra clothes and take them to a second-hand charity shop that can put them to good use. Return your 'new' wardrobe to the shelves and drawers. Now you're set for part two of the challenge.

Here's the new rule: If something goes in, something must go out. Don't buy any new clothes unless you've decided ahead of time what that new clothing is to replace. As clothes deteriorate, that choice is pretty simple. Perhaps it is more difficult when fashions change. And you can't abandon the rule at Christmas or on your birthday. Take a hard look at those three brand-new sweaters and four shirts, or two new handbags and three new dresses. What will they replace? You may end up giving away the new items to OXFAM (they'll enjoy the switch), or you may part with something on the shelf.

Let's summarise the benefits: You've given some pretty nice clothes to people who need them, you're practising self-control in your spending habits (an important skill for stewards) and perhaps you've even donated money that you would have spent on new clothes to an organisation working for those less fortunate than you.

3

Change the Channel

We can act only upon what we know. Because of that fact, we've devoted an entire section of this book to education about hunger. Some of our education on the needs of the world fits neatly, however, into our lifestyle—watching television.

Television can be our friend or our enemy in relation to hunger—our friend if we use it to teach and sensitise us, our enemy if we use it to shut the world out of our lives.

Take Stock

Make a simple time sheet, and for one week record on it all the programmes you watch. Write down the type of programme it was and the total time it took. At the end of the week, categorise your viewing by subject and count up the total amount of time spent on each category. (For example: comedies, seven hours; news, three hours; cartoons, two-and-a-half hours; films, six hours; soaps, twelve hours; sports, twelve-and-a-quarter hours.) After you get over your depression, you're ready for action.

Make Your Move

For some genetic reason outside our control we have to sit on the sofa for several hours each week and look at that little box. The trick now is to change the channel. Specifically: Plan your viewing to include a couple of good hours of educational programmes. Check your television guide at the beginning of the week to see how you need to plan your viewing.

If you have family, include the children in the viewing. They will discover that you take world hunger seriously, they will understand the issues more clearly as you send money to organisations fighting hunger and they'll discover that television goes deeper than *Neighbours, Mutant Hero Turtles* and *The Return of the Three-Headed Gargantuan*. And sometimes these hunger-education programmes will provide you with additional lifestyle options for your response.

By far the most important benefit of changing the channel is that you are regularly taking in a diet of what is really going on in the world. Gradually that awareness becomes assimilated in your very approach to daily living, and, as a consequence, you more naturally choose options that are sensitive to the hungry.

4

Give a Cup of Water

Every day, right outside the offices of a medium-sized church in Los Angeles, hundreds of men line the pavement hoping for construction foremen to drive by and hire their services for the day. These men moved to the USA in search of a better life; months later they are still unemployed, and their families suffer poor living conditions, undernourishment and no medical attention.

You cannot love Jesus and just ignore the hungry, so this church started a very simple ministry. Every Saturday, church members make hundreds of ham-and-cheese sandwiches, drive along the pavement and distribute the food free of charge. No strings attached. They've been doing this for more than two years now, and as you might imagine, they have become much more involved in these men's lives—helping the families find housing, employment and medical care and teaching them the skills that will help them thrive in the city of Los Angeles.

Jesus said, 'Whatever you did for one of the least of these brothers of mine, you did for me.' This church takes sandwich-making seriously.

Take Stock

Join up with a couple of others from work or from your church or fellowship. Drive around your town and find out

19

where the hungry are. If you're having trouble getting the information, do a little research: Talk to agencies in your area that work with the needy. The Salvation Army might be a good starting point. Then look at your diary to see if you can set aside one block of time each week.

Make Your Move

Talk with your local supermarket to see if you can get fillers for sandwiches at a discount for the hungry. Make it a fun time with your friends once a week when you make the sandwiches and distribute them. Or perhaps your town has a soup kitchen, or lunch club, that operates every night. Volunteer your services for one night each week.

Some students at Westmont College in the States were creative enough to approach a local coffee shop with their idea: How about turning the little restaurant into a soup-and-sandwich kitchen one night each week? The Christian owner liked the concept, and every Tuesday night dozens of street people were served a delicious meal prepared by college students. The men and women were not expected to sit through a gospel presentation before eating, but, predictably, friendships were fostered over time that resulted in many decisions for Christ as well as opportunities for employment and housing.

5

Gift-O-Mania

What do you give people who already have everything they need? How do you celebrate birthdays and Christmas without breaking the budget and ignoring the hungry?

One of the evidences that we live in a materialistic society is the value placed on the sorts of things we're expected to buy for others. We quickly judge others by what they give us, or we feel uncomfortable if our gifts don't match the 'quality' of other gifts being passed out around the Christmas tree.

Giving gifts is a wonderful way of expressing love and friendship. No need to back away from it just because negative forms are pressing in on us. Rather, we can pursue a higher goal.

Take Stock

Make a list of all the people who are likely to receive gifts from you over the next twelve months. Include all occasions— for example, Christmas, birthdays, weddings, anniversaries, Valentine's Day, and so on. As you think about your commitment to the poor, decide on an amount you feel comfortable spending on gifts. Then begins the adventure of purposeful, directed giving.

Make Your Move

Wonderful art pieces and craftwork, made by people less wealthy than ourselves, are available through catalogues and

shops run by groups such as OXFAM and Tear Fund. These
organisations import directly from artisans in the Third
World, and consequently your purchase does double duty:
It gives a gift and it puts money into the hands of the working
poor. Such gifts range from earrings to beautiful paintings,
weavings and pottery. Usually your purchase comes with a
brochure explaining how the sale of it benefits people in need.
Refer to the list below.

Other gift-giving ideas you might try:

- Instead of giving gifts to everyone, draw names among family
  members and relatives. Agree to abide by the draw. This
  method allows you to buy a gift that is carefully matched to
  the person. Consider sending some of the money you saved
  to a relief and development organisation.

- Send a financial gift to a hunger-related ministry in the name
  of a family member. The ministry will send your relative a
  card announcing your gift to the poor (on his or her behalf)
  in celebration of Christmas.

- Purchase gifts that educate regarding world hunger. Possibilities range from colouring books and posters to reference
  materials to videos.

Write to or phone the following organisations for catalogues
or addresses of shops in your area:

OXFAM
274 Banbury Road
Oxford
OX2 7DZ
(0865) 311311

Tear Fund
100 Church Road
Teddington
Middlesex
TW11 8QE
081–977 9144

Christian Aid
PO Box 100
London
SE1 7RT
071–620 0719

6

Feet First

Lessening our dependence on private motorised transport makes a difference to a hungry world. Although the connection isn't immediately obvious, give it a try . . .

- The world does not contain an infinite supply of fossil fuels to support our current energy use. Alternative sources are being researched, but for now we still depend on oil for most of our transportation. As the price of oil increases due to diminishing supply, the first people hurt are the poor. They cannot afford the increases that ultimately show up in the cost of housing materials, clothes, transportation, medical services and utilities.

- World population is growing at a phenomenal rate that is actually quite difficult to comprehend. Within a generation there will be twice as many people as today demanding use of the same limited resources for energy. The cost of fuel-related services will rocket even more, and of course the poor will be the first to suffer.

Take Stock

Log an entire week's worth of travel. Be specific: Where did you go, why did you go there, and how? Now, as you anticipate next week's transport needs, see if there is any way to combine errands or short trips and consider alternative forms of travel.

Make Your Move

Think of your car as the last resort (a near-impossible notion for those living in rural areas, of course). Have to go to the shops? Walk. Many of us live within walking distance of our church, work and our favourite café. It takes a little more time to walk, but mostly it's a matter of a change of habit.

Bicycles are the next best option. A bike can easily get the typical student or adult to a spot four miles away without much trouble or effort; in fact, if you live in a traffic-clogged city, the bike will likely get you to your destination sooner than a car. Some cities offer good public transport via buses and trains. Go out of your way to make use of them, and enjoy your favourite book while your 'chauffeur' fights the traffic. If you simply have to use the car, try to get into a pattern of not doing it alone (very difficult for the fiercely independent).

The benefits of going 'feet first' include saving precious resources, increasing your reading time, getting great exercise, meeting new people and sparing the atmosphere the onslaught of unnecessary air pollution. In addition, you may consider sending some of the money you save to organisations linked to the poor.

7

Tame the Dough

There just never seems to be enough money. And yet most of us would be surprised to see how much of it slips unnoticed through our fingers. Consequently, when we're faced with the challenge of helping the hungry, we're left wishing we 'could afford' to give.

Budgeting can be an excellent tool in taming the flow of our money. It helps us to take control of our spending and feel the satisfaction of putting our money where our heart is. Really, we should think of it as a process that frees us rather than stifles us.

Take Stock

As with the earlier suggestion on recording your TV viewing habits, make up a time sheet and record on it every single penny you spend during an entire month. Make categories for what you anticipate you will spend, and leave space for the unexpected. Every night, before going to bed, enter your totals for that day. Make your grand totals at the end of the month. Your count might look something like this: petrol, £15; haircut, £5; McDonald's, £22; Pepsi, £30; toothpaste, £1.50; other food, £38.

It's good to take an honest look. This is nothing more than a tool—your friend—to help you direct some of your money to the hungry.

Make Your Move

Now all you have to do is decide how much you want to spend on the poor. After you come up with that figure, go through your spending list and decide how much you will cut back in certain categories to come up with that total. (Let's see—reduce 'other food' by £10 per month.) This is a relatively painless method of setting aside money for others; besides, it's good skill development for all areas of your spending.

Choose a worthwhile organisation for your monthly contribution, and enjoy the satisfaction of knowing you're making a difference. Just £15 redirected to a hungry child can produce multiple benefits: food, medicine and education for that child, while you receive the satisfaction of making a real difference through small, personal sacrifices.

The British tax system has three tax schemes which encourage gifts to charity by giving income tax relief. So, for instance, if you donate £60 to a charity, *you* only actually give £45. The other £15 can be claimed back from the Inland Revenue by signing a covenant form to give an annual amount over four years. If you pay tax at the top rate (40% instead of 25%) you can claim another £9 on your donation so that your £60 gift only actually costs you £36.

If you wish, you can choose 'pay-roll giving' if you are an employee. You pick your charity and an amount (up to £50 a month). Then your employer automatically deducts this from your salary before tax, giving you tax relief at your highest rate.

The third alternative is 'gift aid'. Since 1st October, 1990, charities have been able to claim back tax at the basic rate on lump sum gifts under the gift aid scheme, but the minimum amount you can give under this scheme is £400—which, given in this way, is worth £533 to the charity. (Please note that this particular scheme cannot be used for bequests.)

For more information, write to your local tax enquiry

centre, listed separately under 'Inland Revenue—Tax Enquiry Centres' in your local telephone directory.

Leaflets which give more information include: *IR64 1986—Business Tax Relief—Charity Giving; IR65 1991—Individual Tax Relief—Charity Giving; IR75 1987—Guide to Charity Giving; IR113 1990—Gift Aid Guide to Donors.*

8

Working on Leisure

All of us think recreation is important, and a few of us even manage to make time for it on a regular basis. Many of us, however, are recreation bingers. We energetically pursue an idea for a couple of rounds but then drop that pursuit until the next nudge pushes us out of our chair once again. Actually, most of us relax in unconscious ways. We take a stroll down the street, weed the garden, wash the car, sit back and read every article in the latest magazine or sit through an entire two-hour recording of our favourite music.

One way to bring good recreation—or a change of pace, if you will—into our lives is to intentionally and regularly take up activities that link us to the hungry world.

Take Stock

We relax more than we probably realise. In 1985, Americans said they had an average of five-and-a-half leisure hours per day. That is expected to increase to six hours by the year 2000. It is time to log again: Make a complete listing of all your 'free' or 'leisure' hours over a two-week period. Write down with each entry what you did during that time. Examples would include watching TV, reading, aerobics, jogging and listening to music.

Make Your Move

Decide how much time you want to set aside to experiment with leisure-for-hunger. See what you think about these possibilities:

- Ask your church if you can do some gardening or maintenance work for them once a week for a couple of hours at a time. Ask that rather than paying you directly for that work, they put the equivalent wage into a special benevolent fund that can be used at the pastor's discretion for the needy who turn up on the church's doorstep.

- Find out where the elderly of your community live. Become acquainted with a few of them, and volunteer to take one evening each week to do their shopping. Walking down the shopping aisles and up their stairs will get your blood flowing as you minister to their physical need at the same time.

- Wash cars on Saturday mornings and donate the money you make to your local homeless shelter or related organisation. And watch your biceps grow.

- If you're handy with tools, volunteer to spend a few hours each week repairing broken taps, faulty hinges and stubborn latches for people who are stuck in their houses or can't afford to pay the regular rates for such work and don't have the know-how.

Use your imagination. The possibilities are endless. Watch the calories leave your body as you take positive steps to fight poverty.

9

Double Your Money

Typically, Westerners require much more money to operate in ministry than do people from other parts of the world. For example, the average Western missionary family may require an annual salary of £20,000 to work in Swaziland, Africa. That's more money than the Swazi prince makes. On the other hand, that same £20,000 could support ten Swazi families full-time during the same year.

This doesn't negate the value of missionaries—some are needed for their special gifts and the contributions they can make in cross-cultural ministry. But our giving can go much further if we include nationals, who understand their needs more clearly and who can accomplish the same work for much less.

Take Stock

If you give money to mission work, you are also helping to fight poverty. All of the gospel's work in some manner reduces human suffering. Make a list of all the money you give to missions, both in Britain and abroad. Perhaps you give through your church or directly to organisations based in Britain. Consider how much you'd like to redirect to national-run ministries.

Make Your Move

Below are listed four organisations for starters. All of these ministries are run by nationals. Their ministries demonstrate concern for people's physical and spiritual needs alike. They would gladly receive your financial contributions. You might investigate other possibilities as well. Write to the organisations and tell them you want to begin regular donations to their work (give them an idea of how much you're hoping to give). Ask them for the best way to send money to them and for a brief description of what primary need they would prefer your gifts to support.

Asia
Ajith Fernando
Youth for Christ
PO Box 1311
Colombo
Sri Lanka

Vishal Mangalwadi
105 Savitri Commercial
  Complex
Greater Kailash II
New Delhi 110048
India

Africa
Caesar Molebatsi
Youth Alive Ministries
PO Box 129
Orlando 1804
Soweto
Republic of South Africa

Latin America
Revd Pedro Arana
Misión Urbana y Rural
Apartado 21–0005
Lima 21
Peru

10

Alternative Holidays

Here's a simple one. Common sense tells us that life requires some times of relaxation—planned holidays. Some of us spend a week hiking round the country, or staying at a holiday camp in a coastal town. A few of us may be lucky enough to spend a month in another country, meeting new people, eating strange foods and learning fascinating customs that are not parts of our own culture.

Take Stock

There is no good reason to give up these holidays. They restore our bodies, expand our worldview and give us courage to face the boss for another few months. But how about *adding* a couple of short bonus holidays to your life each year? Look at your calendar for the next twelve months. Are there any weekends that are free? Any that you could mark on your calendar in advance for an alternative holiday? The answer is probably yes, and if you block out a couple of weekends now they won't fill up later with unplanned diversions.

Make Your Move

Do some research. Ask at your church, town hall or library. Ask where you could go for a weekend to learn more about the world's needs. Perhaps it could be helping at an inner city play group, a pensioners' lunch club, a homeless hostel or a youth club. Any number of inner city churches run such groups and are often grateful for volunteers. Choose a place close enough for you to be able to reach it after work Friday night. Stay there till Sunday afternoon.

The benefits should be pretty obvious: You will get a change of pace, learn something new and reinforce your sensitivity and commitment to hunger-related needs. Broaden your scope of options for effective involvement. Take the chance. Go to your calendar and mark on it two weekends over the next twelve months. If it helps, call a friend and plan your alternative holiday together.

11

Sponsor a Child

'Sponsoring' a child may be the most common response we have all learned to world hunger. Several organisations are expertly poised to meet the needs of people who are suddenly caught in the tragedy of famine, floods, earthquakes or war, and these same organisations make it their business to take on long-term development projects that work in partnership with communities in need. For as little as £10 to £15 a month, you can help towards the cost of providing a child in Africa, Asia or Latin America with all the nutrition, education and medical attention he or she will need in the tender years.

Take Stock

Few of us know a hungry child personally. Hunger is a distant, nameless tragedy that seems far removed from our immediate environment. In fact, we just cannot imagine our next-door neighbour's children dying from lack of food. Child sponsorship schemes can help us ask the basic question: Do I know hunger by name? The one great benefit of child sponsorship (other than the obvious and immediate value to the child) is that the sponsor receives a picture of the child, complete with name and history. That little child personalises hunger, helping us to realise more acutely the offence that hunger brings to the world. If you do not know any hungry persons by name, consider child sponsorship.

Make Your Move

We have listed Tear Fund as one organisation that is involved in child sponsorship. Write to them and they will send you a photo of a child whom you can support each month. There are many other excellent organisations involved in child sponsorship. Perhaps your own denomination has such a scheme.

Tear Fund
100 Church Road
Teddington
Middlesex
TW11 8QE
081–977 9144

12

Foster Care

Today there are 325,000 foster children in the United States alone. The majority of them are victims of cruel circumstances that may include sexual or emotional abuse, loss of parents through death, or poverty that renders parents incapable of caring. Some of these children are the result of teenage pregnancies in which the mother decided against an abortion.

Take Stock

We must ask, 'Where do all these children go?' A foster child is a ward of court, meaning that he or she is officially cared for by the state. The courts decide where these children go, and unfortunately, there are only 125,000 homes in the United States that currently open their doors to foster children. It needn't be so. In America, there is one church for every foster child. Christians there—and in Britain as well—could reach out and minister to the 'least of these'.

Make Your Move

Foster care is obviously more demanding of our time and energy than sponsorship. But if Christians take on this need *together*, these children can have loving homes. Our suggestion is that you approach your church leadership and explore the idea that the church adopt the goal of always having at least one foster child in the congregation. Because this commitment is a significant one for a family to make, the church could create a support group of members interested in foster care. The group's commitments would include providing tangible support to the family that takes in the foster child. The group's members could also take a special interest in the foster child.

Check with your local social services for information on foster care. Each authority has its own regulations and guidelines. Or you can contact, for further information:

Revd Bill Lynn
National Children's Home Pastoral Director
85 Highbury Park
London
N5 1UD
071–226 2033

Barnardo's
Tanners Lane
Barkingside
Ilford
Essex
IG6 1QG
081–550 8822

13

Adoption

Adopting a child is the ultimate sponsorship approach and obviously the most demanding lifestyle option you will face. Thousands of children will never have a mum or a dad. They will move from foster home to foster home as wards of the court until they reach the age of eighteen. They are orphans. The apostle James says that those who care for orphans practice *pure religion* (Jas 1:27). This form of reaching out to others reflects as perfectly as is possible (to humans) the tender and compassionate heart of God. Our heavenly Father is painfully interested in the plight of orphans.

Take Stock

Perhaps God will lead you to adopt. If you are feeling nudged in this direction, there are a couple of places to begin. Talk with parents who have adopted. You'll hear many heart-warming stories of success, and you'll hear a similar number of stories of hardship and failure. Read about it at your local library, ask the social services office for a meeting with the staff responsible for monitoring adoptions, talk with adoption agencies and talk with kids who were adopted. Search the heart of God, as best you can, to see if you and your spouse should take this step. It will be as big as any step you ever have taken, and it should be mutual and from the bottom of your hearts. Be sure to inquire also about the various financial costs involved with adoption.

Make Your Move

If it still seems to be the direction in which God is leading you, ask your social services about the regulations for adopting in your area. They can give you information on reputable organisations, as can some of your local churches. Consider whether you are willing to take a mixed-race or mildly handicapped child. As we suggested in discussing foster care, see if your local church would be willing to create a support group specifically to care for you and your spouse as you make this important move.

14

Change Your Address

We often carry prejudices and simplistic notions regarding people's poverty because we have very little appreciation for the causes of their pain. The Scriptures tell us that Jesus understands all of our needs because he came to earth and was subjected to all the conditions common to human existence. We are at our most effective when we live among the people whom we hope eventually to serve. The fancy name for this approach is 'incarnational ministry'.

Take Stock

Relocating to these places of pain is no easy challenge. We're not talking about a career change here, but about changing your address while holding on to the same job or continuing your studies. If you would like to consider this option seriously, join up with a couple of friends and take a tour through an area that is obviously more needy. Write down the names of the churches, social agencies and ministries that are located right in the centres of need—they are clearly taking their service seriously. Back home, call the organisations and ask their advice. Tell them what you're thinking and see if they would let you spend half a day with them, talking about life-in-ministry. Make sure you talk with several groups.

Prayerfully consider linking up with one of these churches

or organisations—as a lay person. Don't move into its area yet; rather, make regular visits, volunteering your time in its activities and attending its business meetings or fellowship meetings. In time you will either draw closer to the work or drift away.

Make Your Move

When you sense that the Lord has opened a door to you, seek the support and encouragement of your faithful friends as you relocate. Don't move in with big plans and flashy ideas. Stay linked to the organisation you have come to love, and continue to volunteer under its direction. You may end up implementing many of the ideas we have suggested in this book, and you may eventually work *full-time* [with] the poor in your new location.

There are a number of organisations that are devoted to helping Christians who want to relocate to places of special need. Contact them, or your denomination's headquarters, for expert help and fellowship:

Evangelical Alliance
Whitefield House
186 Kennington Park Road
London
SE11 4BT
071–582 0228

Evangelical Coalition for Urban Mission
85a Allerton Road
Liverpool
Merseyside
L18 2DA
051–722 8145

Evangelical Coalition on Drug and Alcohol Abuse
Whitefield House
186 Kennington Park Road
London
SE11 4BT
071–582 0228

The Shaftesbury Society
18 Kingston Road
London
SW19 1JZ
081–542 5550

Oasis Trust
Haddon Hall
22 Tower Bridge Road
London
SE1 4TR
071–231 4583

15

Push Your Pen

The pen is mightier than the sword, we are told. Well, it's true in the case of world hunger. An exciting US Christian citizens' lobbying group, Bread for the World, has a membership of more than 40,000 men and women who regularly write to the President of the United States, their senators and their congress-persons on initatives related to world hunger. BFW has an impressive track record of influencing the nation's lawmakers including bringing about the passage of a congressional bill requiring that millions of bushels of wheat be set aside by the government for disaster relief, and other bills establishing an innovative national nutrition programme for mothers with young children.

Former American president Jimmy Carter is currently heading a bold campaign created by Bread for the World: the Harvest of Peace campaign. The goal is to transfer a percentage of the USA's foreign military assistance to peaceful development projects. According to Arthur Simon, founder of Bread for the World, one trillion dollars is spent annually on the world military—more than the total combined income of the world's poor.

Have you ever wondered how much of your tax money helps the hungry? Or how about the stickiest question: How much of your tax money *contributes* to the creation of poverty? Maybe you could spend time each week writing to Members of Parliament about the issues of hunger

---

and poverty. More Christians need to make their thoughts known. You *can* make a difference by writing.

Movement for Christian Democracy
c/o David Alton, MP
House of Commons
London
SW1A OAA
071–219 3454

16

Punch Those Keys

To most adventurous people, accounting seems a very staid pursuit. Accountants are often unjustly stereotyped as being uninteresting. Of course, we stand against such categorisations and argue that accountants can do some of the most important and exciting work in the church's outreach to the poor.

In one low-cost government housing project in the States, an accountant offered his services to poor people who were having difficulty filling in their income-tax returns. He also worked with the tenants' (residents') community council, helping its members to apply for grants to fund community development projects and cultural enrichment programmes for children. Setting up systems to check expenditures and to maintain fiscal controls for community programmes was another invaluable service he rendered. It can easily be said that this accountant did more, in his 'spare time', to help the poor of this community than all the city-appointed community workers put together.

Take Stock

It should be noted that almost all economic development schemes established in minority communities are suffering because of inadequate accounting services. When checking with the commissions set up to foster minority business, we find with sad regularity that most minority businesses fail. A major cause of this failure is (you guessed it!) poor accounting. Keeping track of stock and outstanding credits, estimating an adequate cash flow and determining proper reserves all require people with accounting skills. If the poor are to organise themselves economically, they will need accountants to work with them, and to train them to do their own accounting well.

Make Your Move

It is time for us to give a warning to avoid the either-or syndrome. Certainly there are full-time employment opportunities for accountants who want to use their skills for the poor. But those who have chosen the typical accounting practice should not shy away from donating time and energy to charitable organisations that need their help. Numerous Christian organisations that work among the poor would have a hard time surviving if they did not receive voluntary accounting help. An annual audit, often required by law, can cost a struggling Christian charity thousands of pounds that it can ill afford to spend.

As a consequence of the recent financial scandals surrounding certain Christian leaders in the States, Christian organisations have been called on by both the government and the Christian community to tighten up their fiscal accountability. This is especially true for those organisations that are doing work among the poor in far-off places such as Haiti. Everybody knows that fraud is easy in such settings, so suspicions are beginning to run high. Accountants can become agents of God, keeping Christian ministries honest and enabling the rest of the Christian community to have trust in them.

17

Tune-Up Masters

This may sound like a strange idea for someone who wants to serve the poor in the name of Christ. But if it does sound strange to you, it is only because you don't know what is going on in the poor sections of our cities. Car mechanics of any kind are hard to find in these areas, and those who do exist are often inept or rip-off artists. A study made some years ago on car mechanics in poor sections of Philadelphia in the States proved that the overwhelming proportion of them cheated their customers. For many of the customers, the cheating amounted to the equivalent of several hundred dollars.

Take Stock

Even those with well-paid jobs know how an unexpected car bill can throw a family budget into chaos. Imagine how exorbitantly high car repairs can devastate a very poor family. A mechanic with a Christian calling can make a difference for them (and can also help community transport groups which rely on old vehicles).

Make Your Move

Find the people in your fellowship who would like to join you in implementing this idea. It's possible to go it alone, but you will have more fun if you can work with others. Get a pad and clipboard and choose a street in a low-income area. Go from house to house and tell the residents that you are offering a low-cost mechanic service to people who would like their vehicles checked over and tuned up. Make up a schedule for one full Saturday. You could offer to do a tune-up and oil change at cost, or you might prefer to figure out how many you can afford to do for nothing.

Too often a £20 problem becomes a mechanic's £200 opportunity. Your simple diagnostic service and repair job can save a poor person from further economic disaster.

Section 2

PRACTICAL IDEAS FOR YOUR CHURCH OR FELLOWSHIP

When individuals get together and combine their vision and energy for the poor, they are a powerful centre of compassion. Their combined efforts make significant dents in the world's hunger and give public testimony to the loving gospel of Jesus Christ.

We hope you'll find our practical ideas helpful and challenging. We have deviated from the old model of go-and-build-an-orphanage-in-some-faraway-spot. Too often that approach suggests to us that hunger is really a distant problem, that we from the West can go 'over there' and easily solve 'their' problems, and it also takes away jobs in construction, plumbing and management that could be creating wealth for the locally impoverished.

Several of the ideas you'll read in this section require just a night, a weekend, a month or a little extra cash. Others, you'll find, will require a major commitment from your fellowship or church that may equal in scope anything you have taken on in the past. We believe that the fellowship of Christians can stand uniquely in the gap; that's why we're willing to offer bold and demanding ways to fight poverty. It's our conviction that the church should lead the way in feeding the hungry, and our hope is that the world will become curious about why it is that we so wholeheartedly and enthusiastically go about it.

A brief warning regarding church 'missions programmes'. Don't let the programme itself become the objective. Merely occupying a place in the church budget is not a worthy goal. Serving and learning from the disadvantaged is your purpose.

Keep the organising work lean and focused; don't bite off more than you can chew. For example, if your Sunday school class decides to help abused women and children, start by finding out about local needs and the services that exist to meet these needs. You may arrive at the point of actually providing shelter, but it is possible that the most important contribution your group can make is some other form of assistance. Start with reasonable goals, proceed cautiously and stay together.

The programme must have a *personal* effect, or it is a waste of everyone's time. It should tangibly help the disadvantaged (Bible study is the right place to start, but love in action is what the gospel is all about). And the programme should be a context in which the Holy Spirit will work in your life. The purpose is to be transformed into the image of Christ—and to participate as that transforming power makes a difference in the lives of those suffering from injustice.

Give credence to the emotional risks relatively well-paid Christians face when working with poor people. It can be frightening to work with those very different from ourselves (at least that's how we perceive them in the beginning). Urban aesthetics are different from those of the clean suburbs. The challenges of poverty are overwhelming in many respects. We must allow ourselves and those in our group to find out how to cope internally. It will be hard enough to recruit people for the group—don't burn them out. One chief outcome of group initiatives is the love you develop for one another in the process. God is not honoured if we serve the poor while damaging our own relationships. Be gentle.

18

Day Care

It is a painful fact of contemporary life that a significant number of children have to be in day-care centres. A growing number of empirical studies back up the idea that it is better for children to be under the care of their own parents during their early years of development. But for a very large proportion of parents, and particularly for poor parents, day care is not a choice but a necessity. Consequently those who most imprint the minds of children are those who run the growing number of day-care centres. It is obvious how important it is that lots of these day-care workers be Christians.

Many churches are responding to the need for day care in their communities. This is good because it enables churches to be better stewards of their underused buildings, and it also provides them with an excellent opportunity to establish relationships with community people. Undoubtedly a significant number of persons who take advantage of the day-care services provided by churches end up being incorporated into the worship and life of those churches. We would like to see evangelistic outreach coupled with day-care services, but even when such is not the case churches would do well to provide day care. It is one of the best ways to assist the working poor. Good day care helps the poor to rest in the confidence that their children are receiving the best and most loving care possible.

Most congregations have adults who work primarily from

the home or who are retired. And most churches have the physical space needed for a good day-care service. The simple way to proceed with this idea is to call a meeting of members who see the value of day care. Determine how many adult hours could be volunteered each week, what the costs related to day care would be and what national and local regulations apply. You may be able to charge a modest fee to each family using the day care and thus support one full-time staff worker, who then co-ordinates all the volunteers.

19

Latchkey Care

Too many children have nowhere to go to after school. Their parents work full time and so they are left with no protection or supervision for several hours each day. It is during this vulnerable time that children find themselves most susceptible to drug abuse, sexual abuse and gang activity.

In the States, the Evangelical Association for the Promotion of Education (EAPE) is a missionary organisation that has made the establishment of after-school latchkey facilities a major part of its urban outreach. Using church buildings located in poor neighbourhoods, it has set up ten of these facilities and through them provides supervised care for children of working parents. The children are involved in a variety of activities that include Bible study, singing, games, crafts and teaching. They are kept in a safe environment until their parents finish work and are able to come and get them. Equally significant, what goes on at these latchkey facilities has had a measurable impact on the academic success of the children who attend.

Implementing this idea is best pursued in the manner described in the previous discussion, 'Day Care'. If a church is unsure of its ability to implement a day-care service, a latchkey service is a good starting point because the demands are not as significant. A latchkey service could become a test case for your fellowship group's ability to expand its ministry into a full day-care service sometime in the future. But do make sure you are fully aware of the implications of the Children's Charter (available from Her Majesty's Stationery Office).

20

Shelters for the Homeless

The number of people who wander aimlessly on the streets of our cities is increasing dramatically. The causes are many. In America, as in the UK, some of the homelessness is the result of a court-ordered deinstitutionalisation of the mentally ill. The United States Supreme Court has ruled that those with emotional or psychological problems who are not a danger to themselves or to society cannot be institutionalised against their will. Consequently, tens of thousands of persons who a decade ago would have been in psychiatric hospitals are now on the streets.

Another relatively recent cause of homelessness is related to drugs. Addicts often give up house and home to get the money to feed their habit. At times other members of their families are made homeless because of them. But none of this should minimise our awareness that there is an increasing number of homeless people who are just plain poor and cannot secure affordable housing.

Those who are willing to provide shelters for the homeless will find that there is government money available for the services such shelters provide. We need people motivated by love for Christ and the poor. The opportunities are there, but they take time.

To implement this idea you need two elements: a building that can accommodate several beds (male and female facilities), a kitchen and bathrooms; and a volunteer staff that will work with two goals in mind—caring for the immediate needs of the homeless and looking, with them, for long-term solutions.

Your town may already be caring for the homeless. If so, see if they need help and if in fact they are adequately reaching the homeless of your region. If help is needed, join in.

If there isn't anything set up in your town, see if you can bring together *several* local churches that will own the goal. This is the place to find the volunteers. Among the churches you should be able to come up with enough funds to hire a full time co-ordinator. Then approach local businesses. Any large town has vacant or underused buildings that could serve as shelter facilities.

There are few business leaders who do not understand the value of caring for the homeless. Show them the united effort of the churches to *staff* the effort, and challenge them to provide and equip the *facility*.

Finally, approach organisations such as The Lions and Rotary Club with a very simple *food* budget. Ask them to take on the third dimension of making this effort for the homeless a success. Many times you will discover that members of these clubs run local grocery shops and restaurants. They could easily be a part of the solution.

For advice, contact:

Adullam Homes Housing Association Ltd
11 Park Avenue
Hockley
Birmingham
B18 5ND
021–554 9777

Oasis Trust
Haddon Hall
22 Tower Bridge Road
London
SE1 4TR
071–231 4583

Evangelical Alliance
Home Affairs Department
Whitefield House
186 Kennington Park Road
London
SE11 4BT
071–582 0228

21

Build Homes

Obviously, the idea of building homes goes a step beyond providing shelters, and it requires a lot more work. One reason people remain homeless is that they are just not able to pay the exorbitant rents that are often charged in the low-income districts of cities. Finding a new home is no easy matter. Missing your rent payment was a result of being low on funds. Now you have to find a new place and pay not only your first month's rent up front but also an equivalent 'final month's rent' and a security deposit.

Landlords in the inner city do not have a reputation for keeping their flats or houses in good shape. Rats, broken taps and windows, cockroaches and clogged toilets are all too common. An interesting response to these conditions is growing in the US city of Los Angeles, where judges are requiring these 'slum lords' to live in their own flats or houses as punishment for not bringing their buildings up to sanitary and safe city-code standards.

You can do something about this problem. Adullam Homes has taken the long view on the problem of homeless-ness. This organisation links local Christians with hostels for the homeless. This involves Christians befriending residents and getting involved in support for them and staff. And one example is Christians forming building repairs groups to do repairs and building work, purely for the cost of materials, where it would be impossible for repairs and maintenance to

be done any other way. Often, Christian professional trades-
men will give time to worthwhile projects for nothing, as
long as they are not undermining their own business.

   Adullam has many success stories. Its track record is good,
and its people are ready to help you co-ordinate such a project
in your region. You can begin by contacting them; they will
help you and your fellowship get involved.

   Adullam Homes is a registered housing association. Many
denominations have their own. Housing associations are
groups of at least eight people (including a secretary) who
come together to provide either new or converted housing
for themselves or others. They are non-profit-making and
have to be registered with the Register of Friendly Societies.
Housing co-operatives are a specialised form of housing
association whose aim and function is to provide homes for
their members. They also must be registered with the Register
of Friendly Societies.

Adullam Homes Housing Association Ltd
11 Park Avenue
Hockley
Birmingham
B18 5ND
021–554 9777

22

Create a Lunch Club

In the lifestyle section, we suggested that you volunteer once a week at a soup kitchen or lunch club, or see if you can create one at a local restaurant.

Churches are uniquely placed to run lunch clubs. Most already have a pretty nice commercial-sized kitchen plus a fellowship hall with plenty of sitting room. Operating a lunch club each day in a way that provides inexpensive, nutritious food, with dignity, is a superb way to care for the poor.

Don't be humdrum about it—use your imagination. Give your club a name, such as 'Sophie's Corner'. Create a simple menu of soup, sandwiches and beverages, and paint a board displaying the options. Have a pay-as-you're-able policy, but suggest prices, such as ten pence per sandwich and five pence per cup of soup or drink. Talk to your local grocer to see about purchasing the food in bulk and at cost. You might even check your local borough council for surplus EEC cheese, butter and beef.

No need to go it alone. Consult with a few other local churches. Perhaps they'd be willing to join the effort by supplying volunteers to help with preparation and serving; they might even be willing to provide funds. Getting the word out to the hungry is easy enough. Contact all the local churches, borough councils and service organisations, describing your lunch club. Put an ad in the local free paper, and let the heads of local schools know. They often are most aware of the poverty from which some of their pupils come.

Let 'Sophie's Corner' provide an upbeat atmosphere. Decorate the room with bright colours, play recorded music in the background and consider including a weekly talent night. Most churches have aspiring musicians who would love to give the public a taste of their goods. If you're having trouble locating such talent, contact Christian Unions at nearby colleges and ask their students to sign up.

Be careful not to create an 'entrapment' environment— where people feel they have to sit through a gospel presentation in order to eat. In time, those who genuinely want to know more about Jesus will ask.

23

Provide a Teaching Service

Too many poor children just do not have a solid chance of getting ahead. They go to school tired (having slept in crowded quarters) and hungry. They're listless during much of the school day and miss many critical ideas in the learning process. Back home there is nowhere to do homework, and perhaps no help from parents who left school early. These students are destined to a downward spiral that will result in leaving school early and failing to acquire the skills of reading, writing and maths. They will be underemployed and will follow their parents into the cycle of poverty.

Your church or fellowship probably has many who are college educated, and maybe even teachers. You will need the guidance of trained teachers in planning curriculum and training the other volunteers. With help from your local schools, you can discover what specific needs children in the area have, and then you can make people aware of your services, offering courses that fit needs. Typically a teaching session will last forty-five minutes to an hour per day. You can do small class sessions and one-to-one work, depending on the needs of the pupils. Teachers in the local schools will love you for it, and so will the parents; but most of all, you will be preparing a child for a good future.

Incidentally, the teaching service is a marvellous addition to the latchkey service, because you will often discover that the same children who need latchkey care are those who will benefit from teaching.

24

Professional Intervention

Often poverty strikes through a series of errors: A rent cheque bounces, a poll tax payment is missed and car insurance lapses—all in the same week. You bump into someone's car at a crossroad; before you know what's happening you are arrested, and while you are on remand awaiting your hearing your family is evicted from the house. And your boss fires you for missing work four days in a row (you were in prison, of course).

This is no far-fetched scenario. We've seen it far too many times. Often the people most hurt in these situations are poor immigrants or inner-city residents.

Several inner-city churches have taken on the challenge of providing professional intervention for times such as these, and because they are known for such ministry, the needy contact them in times of trouble. There are wonderful success stories of pastoral staff asking landlords to be patient for a few more days, convincing employers to rehire the labourer, and providing a character reference to the judge on behalf of the imprisoned so that he or she can get back to work and family. All of us have experienced the grace of Jesus during some rather desperate moments. The church, of all groups, should be sensitive to the need of the poor to receive grace in these potentially devastating situations.

This professional intervention has one other good application in a less critical moment. Some churches will intervene for tenants when repairs are not being made by landlords. Often the problem is nothing more than a language barrier or the tenant's ignorance of a landlord's obligation to repair faulty toilets and exposed wiring. Nothing works as well in these situations as a friendly letter (typed on official letter-head) to the landlord regarding 'my good neighbour Mrs Smith, who seems to be having trouble getting the toilet repaired. I explained to her that it must be a simple misunderstanding. Please do call me at——so that I can assure her you will be attending promptly to her need'.

The most simple way to organise around this service is to designate the church secretary to hear and record the complaints. (You won't need much publicity once the idea reaches the poor.) Form an 'intervention committee' from your church, consisting of lawyers, police officers and social workers who meet regularly to discuss and act upon these needs. In time your operation will become smooth enough to direct most needs immediately to the appropriate commit-tee members without waiting for a regularly scheduled committee meeting.

25

Language Classes

Poverty, in some cases, is no more complex than the inability to speak and read the official language fluently. We are blessed to have dozens of languages represented in our cities. We are much the richer for it because of the cultures and variety these people bring to us.

Unfortunately for many of them, it can take a whole generation before the children are ready to help the family with their English skills. But you can help bridge the gap. You can establish a language class.

Do some research to find out the needs in your town. Again, take advantage of public institutions that are already in touch with these people. Once you sign up people who want to acquire English skills, find the required number of teaching volunteers who have the qualifications (go to other fellowships, if necessary). Someone with formal training in teaching English as a second language is needed to co-ordinate the operation and train volunteers. Such training can often be obtained at your local school or college. Of course, it will be beneficial to learn as much as possible about the culture(s) of the people whom you'll be serving.

When you are ready to schedule the weekly lessons, keep in mind that a successful operation will also depend on the availability of child care and transport; these are areas of service for those volunteers who are not trained in teaching English.

The language service should generally be two-pronged: formal in-class learning, where the students learn the basics of reading and writing, and out-of-class learning, where students learn the language of commerce and transportation. The latter involves trips to the local grocery shop and bank—where the instructor describes the process of buying and banking—and visits to the zoo, recreation centres, the bus depot and local government offices. All too often your students will have been shut out from these services simply because they are unaware of them or, because of language barriers, unable to use them. The more they are able to venture out on their own the less dependent they will be, and ultimately the less vulnerable they will be to circumstances that lead to poverty.

Make sure these classes have an end date. The students can then sense their progress and become motivated by the momentum of getting through a simple curriculum. Have a certificate and awards dinner at the end of the course, and offer students the chance to sign up for the next level of language learning.

Members of one small congregation in California implemented this simple plan, and to their surprise many of the students began attending their church. The word got out to the refugee community that this church was a friendly, helpful group of people, and the growth of the congregation was so dramatic that within eighteen months they were looking for a new meeting place.

Adult literacy and numeracy centres exist in all local authorities in the United Kingdom. Details can be obtained by contacting your local education authority. The authorities are constantly on the lookout for voluntary teachers.

26

Medical Clinics

One of poverty's disquieting choices is between food and medical attention. It's that painfully simple: The £30 goes either to this week's food supply or to the antibiotic for one child's illness.

Most doctors will tell you that many major medical problems are preventable with careful and regular medical attention on the front end of physical ailments. People who do not receive the proper nutritional, sanitary and medical care up front—especially if they are poor—are certain to face severe problems when the ailments come in full force. And because the poor family's life is already so tenuous, additional prescription charges, dental bills and private treatment to avoid long waiting lists can push them over the edge to the worst forms of destitution.

Churches can co-operate by sponsoring day medical clinics and advice centres in the areas where the poor live (transport might be a problem for many of them). The hours of the clinic should run at least from the afternoon to early evening, to accommodate those who work late. Doctors and nurses from several churches can pool their skills and volunteer hours; thus a group can easily operate a clinic where each person's services are required only a few hours per week.

Just think back to the times you have been gripped with panic over your young child's high fever and listlessness, and you will quickly appreciate the fear of a parent caught in similar circumstances who has no immediate access to medical care. It can take days to get an appointment in many inner-city medical centres.

These same clinics could provide prenatal services and infant care. Most of poverty's ills begin in the womb and during the first years of life. Given that many mothers currently receive inadequate prenatal care and advice, there would be no end to the value of this service in your community of need.

Doctors who already have their own practice can operate under their business licence, or your fellowship can create a non-profit company specifically for the purpose of bringing medical care to the poor. These same doctors can advise you of any legal requirements related to providing medical services.

For further information contact:

Christian Medical Fellowship
157 Waterloo Road
London
SE1 8XN
071–928 4694

27

Start a School

It's difficult to understand why the world's most technologic-
ally and democratically advanced nations have yet to work
out how to provide quality education for their children. Many
schools are places of violence and drug abuse where small
children feel they have done well each day if they have simply
managed to survive the gang warfare and dodge the drug
barons. We should be able to do better.

Some middle class and wealthy churches have responded
by starting their own schools, in order to provide their
children with the protection they need in their vulnerable
years as well as quality educational experiences. Unfortunately,
too many of these Christian schools abandon the poor in the
process.

Creating a school is an enormous task that requires careful
planning, significant fund-raising and a long start-up period.
Still, many churches have worked out how to do it and provide
a wonderful service for their children. If your town has a
successful church/school programme in effect already, see if
your fellowship could offer its services to ensure that the
poor are included. If no such school programme exists, begin
the research: Go to a neighbouring town where a Christian
school is in full swing, and contact your denomination for
references.

The church that has a heart for the hungry will insist that
its school programme is not a place to escape the world, but

rather a place to take leadership in reaching out to the world. Registration policies could require that at least half of the student body be made up of children who cannot afford a private education. Tuition could be based on a graduated scale that reflects ability to pay, and parents could be encouraged to contribute their time to classroom and playground duties if their workload allows.

Again, there is no reason for a church to go it alone. Because Christians believe in Jesus' prayer that we work in unity, why not link six or seven churches together to provide quality private education to the poor? Agree together that you will not grow any faster than your ability to retain a student body made up of at least fifty per cent of students from the hungry side of town. What a beautiful and satisfying way to end the cycle of poverty.

For more information, contact:

Christian Schools Campaign
Oak Hill School
Okebourne Road
Brentry
Bristol
Avon
BS10 6QY
(0272) 695670

28

Refugee Assistance

Every week refugee families whose lives have been torn apart embark on new lives in Great Britain. They need help with many things, some mundane and some profound. Often they are open to a new spiritual insight. Always they are survivors who have a great deal to teach us.

Sponsoring a refugee family is a ministry which is easy to explain to members of your group and church; the work itself requires little special skill; and the biggest challenge is simply to be there as the family proceeds through the hundreds of adjustments a new life requires.

The opportunity for cross-cultural learning is excellent, and often the major commitment runs its course after a year or so, though you should stay in touch with the family over the long haul if they need you. Of course, refugees have many needs beyond the process of resettlement. Your group may want to become involved with a refugee partner church, learn about advocacy with the refugee community or work on job development with them.

For ideas on working with refugees nearby or overseas, contact the Refugee Advice Support Unit:

Refugee Advice Support Unit
Bondway House
3–9 Bondway
London
SW8 1FJ

Also, the Jubilee Campaign sometimes look for financial help with group action on behalf of refugees:

Jubilee Campaign
PO Box 80
Cobham
Surrey
KT11 2BQ
081–891 5027

29

Prison Ministry

Few forms of service to the disadvantaged have as clear a biblical mandate as outreach to prisoners (see Matthew 25). There are many ministries in Great Britain with an emphasis on prison work; one is likely near you. Some work is organised in the prisons themselves, while other enterprises focus on assisting people after they leave confinement. Still others advocate more humane treatment of prisoners or more just and effective approaches to sentencing.

One of the needs of prisoners rarely considered is their families. Often the one incarcerated is the breadwinner. He or she is unable to provide for the children's food and unable to pay rent. Hunger and homelessness are often linked to prison terms. Loneliness is another consequence. The spouse at home goes to an empty bed every night and gets no adult companionship in the evening.

While such ministry may threaten the average middle class Christian, we would do well to remember that much of the New Testament was written in prison, and we still have much to learn in that context. God is in such a place, and prisoners have great need for basic friendship.

For more information, contact the following:

Prison Fellowship England and Wales
PO Box 945
Chelmsford
Essex
CM2 7PX
(0245) 490249

Prison Fellowship Scotland
PO Box 366
Bishopbriggs
Glasgow
G64 2RF
041–762 4887

Amnesty International
1 Easton Street
London
WC1X 8DJ
071–413 5500

30

Help Stop Domestic Violence

Imagine coming home from school every afternoon to the fists of an ill-tempered parent consumed by alcohol and defeat. Imagine the fear of a teenage daughter who every night has to wonder if Daddy will visit her bedroom again. Imagine being the spouse who fills the roles of cook, cleaner, gardener, sex slave and punch-bag.

In every community women and children live with the fear of abuse and the scars of past abuse. They need protection, advocacy and other forms of assistance. This option for group involvement is close and personal, and all of our towns, our churches, even some of our own homes suffer from this violence.

There are not many opportunities to serve the powerless closer to our own front door. If we focus on achievable goals, rescarch local needs and services and learn from those already involved in ministry among abused persons, we will find a way to reach out tangibly and sensitively to victims and perpetrators.

Find people in your community who understand and address these issues. New Beginnings is an organisation that counsels adult survivors of child abuse and provides support for families and ministers. The Incest Help Line and Support Group was set up to bring wholeness and healing from damaged emotions caused by childhood sexual abuse.

New Beginnings
20 Stratford House
Sackville Street
Southsea
Hampshire
PO5 4BX
(0705) 730250

Incest Help Line and Support Group
PO Box 42
Grantham
Lincolnshire
NG31 6AA
(0476) 66606

Women's Aid Federation
PO Box 391
Bristol
BS99 7WS
(0272) 633542

31

Run a Video Service

A primary form of entertainment for poor people is watching films on video cassette. The reason we are suggesting that your group consider the option of running a video club is that there is a need to provide decent videos for them. There are so many videos which highlight violence and are pornographic; surely Christians see the need for the kinds of videos which promote the values and themes that are at the heart of the gospel. The poor do not live by bread alone. Certainly, providing good entertainment that elevates the soul can easily be seen as a Christian calling.

Don't forget the children. Parents of young children need breathing space. They are often frustrated by the lack of healthy, child-focused videos. One good educational video per day can provide a great benefit to a child's development and a welcome oasis to a parent.

The club can be operated straight from the church. Be sure to protect the video use for those who really need it—otherwise you could end up just serving your own interests. Contact distributors of good viewing and explain your plans; they may give you a good deal. Or see if your local library is willing to provide the video service. If so, your group, together with several others in town, could agree to buy videos for the library. The library takes on the expense of *running* the operation, while you provide the quality material. Ensure that in doing so, you meet the copyright requirements.

32

Entrepreneurs for Biblical Justice

It is time for the church to undertake what may be one of the most relevant ways to help the poor: creating jobs through the establishment of cottage industries and small businesses.

When there were no hospitals, the church created hospitals. When there were no schools or universities, the church created schools and universities. When there were no means of caring for orphans, the church established orphanages. Now the poor cry out for jobs, and a church that listens to people and responds to their needs must get into the task of job creation.

The need for this bold new venture is obvious. The government, which once created new jobs, cannot be expected to do so alone any longer. At both local and the national level, the government is in debt. It is going to be forced to cut back and will be contributing former employees to the growing ranks of the unemployed. Government will not be contributing to job creation in the decades that lie ahead.

The private sector does not offer much hope either. It is true that hundreds of thousands of new jobs were created during the 1980s, but those jobs were, for the most part, very low-paid positions in the service sectors of the economy. While these new low-paid jobs were being created, hundreds of thousands of high-paid jobs in the steel and car industries were lost. Unskilled and semi-skilled labourers who lost

81

high-paid jobs in manufacturing became poor when their only option was minimum-wage employment.

The opportunity and timing for the church to foster job creation through entrepreneurship could not be riper. Churches, many of them located in areas of high unemployment, have buildings with ample space to house small businesses and industries. There are committed Christians in both inner-city and suburban churches who have the needed expertise to serve as consultants for church-sponsored business enterprises.

It is possible for a church to serve as an 'incubator' to several businesses simultaneously. Among the economic ventures which it could sponsor with a high probability of success are the following:

- *A moving business*. In the early stages the church can provide phone answering services, thus cutting overhead costs. Vans can be rented when needed. Promotion of the business can be done through the church, since approximately one out of ten church members moves each year.

- *A cleaning business*. The workers in such a business must be trained if the work is to be done properly. As that training is accomplished, such a business can be co-ordinated with suburban churches, which often have members who need the services of a cleaning company. A lawn-mowing business can be created just as easily.

- *Rebuilding burnt-out alternators and starter motors for cars*. The technical skills required for this work are minimal and easily learned. It is possible that teachers from the local college would be willing to provide the necessary instruction. Through arrangements with local car dealers, the burnt-out alternators and starter motors can be provided. And these same dealers can provide a market for them when they are rebuilt.

The list of possible businesses and industries that could be developed out of the church could go on and on. What is needed is creativity. World Vision in California, USA, provides consulting services to help churches pull off such ventures without losing their tax-exempt status.

Lay people can be located, in sponsoring churches or in nearby suburban churches, who have the skills and experience that the poor who are to own and run these new businesses need. Members of many churches include accountants, solicitors, bankers, marketing consultants and experienced owners of small businesses. Invite such experts to participate in making these entrepreneurial ventures work. It might be the first time their churches have ever called upon them to use their skills so directly in church-related service. Such participation in ministry to the poor would kindle a new enthusiasm for Christian service and also would undoubtedly facilitate major consciousness changes among these 'consultants'.

One is likely to ask why, if the need for job creation by the church is so great, the leaders of the church have not made this endeavour earlier. The answer is quite simple. Christian training colleges have not trained their students to do this kind of work. Many of them have business departments, but they are so busy training young people to take their places in 'establishment' businesses like IBM and GEC that they have ignored the need to raise up those who can enable the poor to become entrepreneurs. Churches at times run football leagues because they have staff members who have taken courses in recreation. Churches often provide counselling services because their ministers are trained in counselling. But when it comes to job creation, churches back off, because pastors don't know how to create small businesses and cottage industries. Lay people do. But the professional staffs of churches consider this sort of thing out of their league.

However, things are changing. At Eastern College in Pennsylvania, USA, graduate programmes have been put into place that are especially designed to prepare students for this calling. Eastern has an MBA programme and a Master of Science programme that get graduates set to go to the poor both in urban America and in Third World countries, to organise indigenous people for entrepreneurial enterprises. The faculty is working on economic development models that can be implemented in impoverished communities so that the poor can have hope for employment.

The seminary related to Eastern College now has a Master of Divinity programme that is training up a new breed of clergy. These new church leaders not only will know how to pastor churches but also will be able to do the kind of job creation we have been discussing. Other Christian colleges are now giving serious attention to the possibilities of getting into economic development for the poor. In the States, it won't be long before many academic programmes like this are in place.

For advice, you could write to:

World Vision (UK)
Dept CO92
Dychurch House
8 Abington Street
Northampton
NN1 2AJ
(0604) 22964

Evangelical Alliance
Christian Initiative Unit
Whitefield House
186 Kennington Park Road
London
SE11 4BT
071–582 0228

33

Serve the Shut-Ins

Many of the elderly poor might be called the 'forgotten people'. They are separated from their families and live in small flats or bedsits in big cities where they are simply unknown. Their age and economic status leave them victims to crooks who would charge them excessively for services, and they are physically vulnerable to bad weather, seasonal viruses and other health threats.

Your group or fellowship has an important calling to serve shut-ins. Locate those in your group who have a sensitivity to the elderly, and go to a block of flats or sheltered housing area where the elderly live. There are several weekly services your group can provide:

- Offer to do their weekly shopping.

- Take them to regularly scheduled doctor visits and help them get prescriptions collected.

- Help them give the bathroom and kitchen a good weekly scrub for mildew and germs.

- Offer to advise them on any sales offers that have come their way during the week—for example, insurance packages.

- Learn the dates of significant family events and help them purchase cards or gifts to send in time. Remember their own birthdays with a card and small gift—or cake and ice cream.

- Provide entertainment by lending them videos, or take them to community events.

Society throws away or ignores the 'useless' people. Christians honour the elderly. What a dignified way to reach out to the poor.

34

Fund-raising Work

All of our suggestions for group efforts involve ways of being personally and directly involved with the poor. This particular idea may or may not involve contact with the poor, but its specific focus is raising money for a well-deserving project that touches the poor.

People who *live* with the poor for the sake of ministry are often overwhelmed by the unending needs that surround them. Not only do these servants constantly *give*, but they also constantly say no, because they are simply unable to meet all the needs that press against their front door. In the lifestyle suggestion 'Double Your Money' (Chapter 9) we offered names of organisations that will make your donations go twice as far as you might expect—if not more. We know that all of them would be greatly encouraged by an occasional large influx of funds to help them meet some of the needs they have to ignore because of financial limitations.

We suggest that twice a year your group arranges a fund-raising work project. It could take two approaches. The first would be to sign up members of the congregation who would like some significant work done in their gardens and are willing to pay for the service, with the understanding that it will benefit the poor. Perhaps you could suggest an amount— for example, £25 per medium-sized garden. If the youth group went after twenty gardens, they could send £500 to a deserving Third World ministry.

The second approach would be to ask the people who are paying you for the work to *double* the amount they pay you— that amount then sponsors your group to do an equivalent amount of work for the elderly poor. The benefits of such a two-pronged approach are numerous:

- The sponsor gets a clean garden.

- The sponsor is blessed to give money that goes to a ministry at double the original fee.

- An elderly couple or individual gets a good service.

- The youth group sweats to raise money for someone 'over there'.

- A Third World organisation is blessed with a significant amount of money.

35

Multi-Ethnic Relationships

If your group chooses to implement several of the ideas we have outlined, members of your fellowship will end up developing close relationships with people of other ethnic backgrounds. A step beyond ministry is developing relationships among peers with differing racial backgrounds. We experience a taste of heaven on earth when we begin to live in loving and accountable relationships with sisters and brothers from other social, economic and ethnic experiences.

A small group with this sort of diversity provides a tremendous opportunity to hear the voice of God in our lives and for our time. Reconciliation, grace, candour and a new and holy energy will emerge from such relationships. At the outset at least, this sort of group initiative will more likely focus on who we are together than on what we do.

Ultimately, concerns of being and identity should take precedence over task. Yes, we should identify and meet needs. But our accomplishments multiply if they grow out of biblical mutuality, in which sisters and brothers freely exercise their giftedness in submission to the Holy Spirit. The Book of Acts tells us this story. We will see even greater things if we serve the Lord and the needy with boldness and humility.

A long-term benefit of multi-ethnic relationships is that we develop the skills of listening more carefully to those who are different from us. Too often the poor are *victims* of our charity rather than beneficiaries. When we have had little contact with people unlike ourselves, we are not able to discern very effectively the best ways of working with others. The poor deserve our best, and the developing of multi-ethnic relationships is an excellent means towards changing *ourselves* for the benefit of others.

Section 3

CAREER OPTIONS

Whatever you are planning to do with your life can be turned into a mission designed to help the poor. Whether your plans are to be in one of the 'professions' or to take up one of the 'blue-collar' vocations, you can make your life's work into service for the impoverished masses who go by the biblical title 'the least of these'.

In living out the high calling of God on behalf of those who seem hopelessly trapped by the ravages of poverty, we would like you to consider some obvious options along with others that may not seem so obvious. As we go over a relatively short list of possible vocations to help the poor, we want you to give special attention to some variants to typical kinds of service. You may discover fresh and creative ways of carrying out the calling to give ourselves to the oppressed. With a little innovation, you can turn some 'ordinary' vocations into radical assignments in God's revolution.

36

Medicine

Let's start with a vocation that comes quickly to mind when we consider going to the poor—medicine. Without doubt there are innumerable places where doctors, dentists and nurses are desperately needed and where missionaries with medical skills can make the difference between life and death for tens of thousands of people.

If you are called to serve in a needy overseas area in some medical capacity, do not let anything we present here dissuade you from this high calling. There are too many missionary organisations whose leaders regularly scan the CVs of applicants hoping to find people who are qualified to be what might be called traditional medical missionaries. But as you think about medical missions, here are some special considerations you might keep in mind.

Stop and think about the fact that most Third World countries have universities which regularly train significant numbers of indigenous people to be doctors and nurses. Unfortunately many of those who graduate from these schools find it impossible to practice medicine in their home country because the people there do not have the means to pay for their services. Often these doctors and nurses must leave their homeland to take advantage of more lucrative opportunities in rich countries like the United States and Canada.

Sometimes indigenous doctors have been known to give

up trying to make their living at medicine because missionary doctors have offered superior services at little or no cost to needy people. In such cases the missionaries could be said to put the indigenous doctors out of business. This sort of thing increases dependency on foreigners and diminishes confidence among native peoples that they can solve their own problems and meet their own needs. But situations like these are not common. Just be aware that such things can happen.

Some of the best medical work being done on the mission field today is being carried out by those who make their contribution by helping indigenous doctors and nurses to do their work more effectively. The Christian Medical Dental Society in the States, for example, sponsors regular short-term mission trips (of two to four weeks) in which Western doctors conduct seminars for indigenous medical professionals, helping them to upgrade their skills and teaching them some of the newest medical discoveries and techniques. Even if you do not feel you should spend your entire life in some Third World country as a doctor or nurse, you should realise that there are important contributions such as these that you can make through short-term service trips.

Then too, in the midst of zealous commitment to 'go where no man has ever gone before' we sometimes fail to recognise that we no longer must go to the Third World in order to go to the Third World. Actually, Third World poverty waits to be encountered in most major cities in the West, including our nation. And in the States, for example, the slums of Brooklyn, the barrios of Los Angeles, the ghettos of Chicago and the government housing projects of Philadelphia are only a few of the places that approximate all the impoverishment and suffering to be found in Third World settings. In these communities the absence of basic medical care is appalling. Sometimes those who live in these places do not know how to gain access to medical services that are available for the poor, but in most instances medical care is simply not available. Missionary doctors and nurses are needed in these places, and you may, upon reflection, consider responding to the needs closest to you as your calling.

Once again, go beyond the 'all-or-nothing' syndrome. Part-time service can be of crucial significance. In Texas, USA, a group of churches set up a clinic for poor people (particularly Mexican migrant workers) and convinced doctors and nurses in their congregations to donate a day a week to do medical missionary work in their own community. The results have been brilliant. This is the kind of thing you might consider doing in a needy community close to where you live or settle down.

Christian Dental Fellowship
136 Kingsway
Woking
Surrey
GU21 1NR
(0483) 715651

Christian Medical Fellowship
157 Waterloo Road
London
SE1 8XN
071–928 4694

37

Law

We all have our lists of lawyer jokes, and in all too many instances the jokes are well deserved. Certainly, in America there are legions of lawyers at work encouraging almost everybody to sue just about everybody. America graduates 40,000 lawyers a year (in all of Japan there are only 16,000 practising lawyers), and far too many of them make a small fortune by creating liability cases that by rights should not exist.

But it is too easy to say simply that there are too many lawyers. In reality, there are too many lawyers for the rich and the powerful and too few available to defend the poor and the oppressed.

If you are planning to study law, consider specialising in individual cases. It will produce less income than working for a commercial company, but then, following Jesus never did carry the promise of lucrative rewards. Here, too, we want to stress that even if you do not make working with the poor a full-time vocation, there is still much that you can do to help poor people.

Several years ago, three lawyers who shared a practice in a small city in West Virginia, USA, heard a sermon that prompted them to see that a commitment to the poor lies at the heart of Christian discipleship. They decided to maintain their regular law practice, but at the same time to put out the word through newspaper ads and announcements on television that they would offer free legal help to people who could not afford to pay. The response was remarkable.

About a third of all their time is now dedicated to helping poor people. What is more, these lawyers can testify that their commitment to the poor has not hurt their wallets. One of the unforeseen consequences of their willingness to serve the poor sacrificially is that people who had failed or refused to pay fees that were owed have been paying their bills. Accounts from years past that these lawyers had never expected to collect are now suddenly being paid up. Former clients feel obligated to 'do what's right' for these lawyers who have become known for the good they do. In addition, a host of new clients have come to these lawyers because of their reputation.

The cases that these lawyers handle for poor people involve not only the deep troubles that the poor often get into because of drugs, crime and domestic conflicts but also cases where the poor have been cheated by shops and tricked into buying things they really do not need or want. There have been many cases of poor mothers who have been unable to get child support from fathers who have shirked their responsibilities. These three Christian lawyers are doing work that needs to be done but never would have been done had they not become committed to the poor.

For fellowship among Christians in the legal profession, contact:

Lawyers Christian Fellowship
71 Riverside Road
Eaglesham
Glasgow
G76 0DE
041–644 5849

38

Police Work

Usually the first persons to arrive on the scene when there is trouble are the police. Whether it is a rape, a murder, a robbery or a case of assault, it is policemen and policewomen who are the first ones victims have to talk to about what happened. All too often there is a difference between the way the police treat the poor and the way they treat the more affluent. The poor are frequently treated condescendingly. Sometimes what has happened to them is not taken seriously. When poor women are raped or beaten the police have been known to pass over the violence as they would not dare to do if the victims were white and middle class. There are tendencies to ignore child abuse and partner abuse as though these things were to be expected among the lower classes.

It is particularly upsetting to discover that the poor themselves generally view the police as their enemies rather than their protectors. Often racial bias enters into relationships between the police and the poor, so that stereotypes are heightened and oppressive behaviour becomes normal.

Clearly, sensitive, trained Christians can make a difference in police work. Let's not kid ourselves that those who believe in Jesus as Lord, Saviour and God will automatically 'do the right thing' in this vocation. Being baptised does not necessarily take care of deep-rooted prejudices or do away with that middle class consciousness that can subtly expect the worst of the poor. Christians who want to make a difference in this line of service should first spend some time serving cross-culturally in an inner-city ministry. This experience will enable them to know themselves in a new way and to understand those who come from another economic sub-culture. They will have to be prepared to deal with situations that middle class people seldom face. But the Jesus who bids us to go into all the world to preach his gospel expects us to invade the world of the poor and 'become all things to all persons so that we might win a few'.

I know of one particular policeman in Philadelphia who exemplifies what we are talking about. His name is Melvin Floyd. Officer Floyd is an African-American Christian who has taken his calling seriously. Working a beat in one of the most run-down and dangerous sections of the city, he has lived out his commitment to Christ in ways that have earned him the highest honours of the community. People have come to know him as a 'man who cares'. He puts in extra hours dealing with the families of victims and offenders, acting as an agent of reconciliation. His efforts in the war on drugs have become legendary. But one of his best contributions is communicating to middle class suburbanites what life is like in the poor sections of the city and enlisting them as volunteer workers. There are teachers, recreation leaders and Bible teachers who work among the poor because this policeman inspired them to do so.

Another example of the way a police officer can live out the gospel can be found in Benjamin Harris. This man *requested* to be assigned to Passyunk Homes, a run-down government housing project in South Philadelphia. He took this assignment because he wanted to make a difference among the socially disadvantaged people who live in these worn-out housing units. And a difference he has made.

He has organised a teaching service for schoolchildren who are having special problems. He has concentrated on prevent-ing school truancy. He has worked with the tenant council of Passyunk Homes to get financial grants to fix up the buildings and improve the appearance of the community.

The police substation out of which Officer Harris operates has become known among the poor people in the vicinity as a place to go when help is needed. He knows where to refer people when they need help. He knows how to talk to troubled teenagers. He is always ready to referee personal disputes. A number of urban missionary organisations have endeavoured to send workers into Passyunk Homes, but none has done the work of being an apostle more effectively than has Officer Harris.

39

Juvenile Protection

Of course, it is prejudicial to assume that the poor are more likely to commit crimes than are the middle class. But it is certainly true that the poor are more likely to end up in jail or in juvenile protection units than are the wealthier of our society. Any decent course in sociology would help you to understand why. We are not able to go into those reasons here. What we do want to make clear is that there are ample opportunities for Christians to invade the criminal justice system and make a difference for Christ.

In the States, organisations such as Youth for Christ have put together special ministries for teenagers who are in trouble with the law. YFC workers have sponsored schemes in which juvenile offenders are released to them to be cared for and supervised. In several instances halfway houses have been set up to provide residential care for teenagers who otherwise would have been put into prison. Endless case studies give evidence that judges in America often put teenagers in prison simply because there is nowhere else to send them. For instance, if a youngster's father has disappeared and his mother is in a drug rehabilitation centre, the judge may prescribe prison only because there are no alternatives. When Christians step forward to help, they will usually find that the courts welcome their assistance. Along with YFC, Teen Challenge, the ministry started by David Wilkerson, has done brilliantly in this regard.

You and some of your Christian friends might organise yourselves to respond to the need for care for juvenile offenders. The first step would be to contact those who run the court system in your community and find out what requirements they have for those who do this kind of work. You will be surprised how minimal those requirements are. Furthermore, you will probably discover that the Home Office will provide significant financial support should you undertake such an effort. We know of several Christian halfway houses for troubled and delinquent teenagers that receive more than enough money to provide staff and care for a host of poor youngsters who otherwise would have become lost in the penal system. Adullam Homes is an example of this in the United Kingdom.

Adullam Homes Housing Association
11 Park Avenue
Hockley
Birmingham
West Midlands
B18 5ND
021–554 9777

40

Social Work

An obvious vocation for those who want to work among the poor is social work. Many Christian colleges in the United States have become aware of the need for Christians in this field and have initiated programmes that provide some of the best training available.

Many churches are now establishing staff positions for social workers. Also, an array of new Christian institutions is being created, including everything from shelters for the homeless to hospices for AIDS victims.

Christians should see the possibilities that exist within government social service agencies. Certainly there will be limitations on articulating the gospel in these agencies, but there are always ample opportunities for expressing God's love in attitudes and actions.

Malcolm X, one of the prophetic voices of the American Black Muslim movement, might not have been lost to Christianity had the social worker who had his mother as a client displayed a Christian style and attitude to her job. In his autobiography, Malcolm X describes how that social worker destroyed the respect he had had for his mother. After his father's death at the hands of a white drunk driver who was never prosecuted, this white social worker was assigned to investigate his family, to see if they qualified for public assistance. During every visit to their home, the social worker took the young Malcolm aside and questioned him about his mother. She asked whether his mother had any lovers and whether she was doing a proper job in raising him and the rest of the children. The questioning degraded his mother in the boy's eyes. As he watched her meekly leave the room during the interrogation, he lost respect for her. But at the same time he hated the social worker for changing his attitude towards his mother. Malcolm X saw that social worker as another white instrument for degrading black people. His rejection of Christianity was in part due to his conviction that it was a religion belonging to the white society that the social worker had helped him to hate.

We have to ask what the historical ramifications might have been had that social worker related to his family in a Christlike manner.

Social Workers Christian Fellowship
35 Market Lane
Blundeston
Lowestoft
Suffolk
NR32 5AN
(0502) 731202

41

Teaching

For those who take the necessary college courses to graduate as teachers, there are brilliant opportunities to serve the poor in schools. The shortage of good teachers in poor communities has become one of the great scandals of our time. It is common for schools located in poor African-American communities to graduate only one-third of all those who enter. Of those who do graduate, a significant proportion may be functionally illiterate. The same poor levels of achievement are reflected in Britain's urban priority areas, particularly in ethnic minority areas. We are not suggesting that poor teaching is the primary cause of this educational tragedy, but we cannot ignore the fact that poor teaching is a major contributing factor.

One Sunday the pastor of an American urban church read this message from a group of concerned students at the local junior high school:

Dear Pastor Campbell,
Please get the people in your church to pray for us here at Sayre Jr. High. Things are bad. The students are always fighting. Policemen patrol the halls and the lunchroom. We all have to walk through metal detectors when we enter the buildings so they can find guns and knives. Most of the good teachers have left and the teachers that remain are very discouraged. We need help.

Letters like this should challenge Christians to meet such needs. Of course it requires heroism to dare to teach in such places, but we follow a Christ who calls us to be heroic for his sake. It seems as though it is easier to get young teachers to volunteer for teaching overseas than to get them to go to the difficult places so close at hand in poor communities throughout our own country.

Christians are often unaware of the opportunities for evangelism that exist within the state school system. For instance, they are usually ignorant of the fact that school facilities can be used during non-teaching hours for Bible study sessions or for Christian Unions.

What also should be acknowledged is that after school hours teachers can spend time with pupils. In that time nobody can stop them from sharing the love and message of Christ. Very often poor children—who, disproportionately to the general population, come from single-parent families—make their teachers into surrogate mothers and fathers. Such children need the guidance and affection that these relationships can provide.

42

Adult Literacy Education

Among the poor, illiteracy is higher than most of us imagine it to be. Many grow up in environments that discourage reading or have special undetected problems that interfere with reading. Fortunately, our political leaders have decided to do something about this problem. There is among government officials a growing awareness that illiteracy among adults contributes to unemployment—and that it diminishes efficiency as well as productivity among those who do have jobs. If we are to remain economically competitive, our leaders tell us, we must educate all of our citizens to read.

In the US, Barbara Bush, as president's wife, made literacy her special concern. She has spearheaded a number of efforts to establish adult literacy education programmes. Consequently, a number of new employment opportunities are opening up in this field. It does not take much imagination to see that such vocational options provide some of the best and most gratifying ways to help the poor, not only in the States but also in Britain.

A man who teaches in a literacy training programme recently said, 'I get more of a thrill out of seeing my students get high school certificates that I got out of getting my own. When the people we teach to read go on to complete their high school education, we always have a special recognition programme for them here at the literacy centre. We do it not only to make them feel good but because it makes *us* feel so good.' Funding for adult literacy centres is relatively easy to secure in most communities. If government agencies are not in a position to provide the necessary grants, then appeals can be made to service clubs like Rotary and Lions. In providing literacy centres, the churches can find another good use for their generally under-used building facilities. British education also encourages return and learn programmes.

As you consider taking the courses necessary to do adult literacy training, remember that there are also many opportunities to use these skills overseas on the mission field. Literacy centres are being set up in a good number of Third World countries, and mission agencies are beginning to look for people who are trained to educate teachers for such programmes. The Evangelical Alliance Literacy Group is working on this issue at the time of writing.

Every local education authority is running adult literacy courses and welcomes volunteers who will sit, listen and encourage people who want to improve their literacy skills.

Evangelical Alliance
Literacy Group
Whitefield House
186 Kennington Park Road
London
SE11 4BT
071–582 0228

43

The Pastorate

Men and women who want vocations that minister directly to poor people should not overlook being a pastor. Churches in poor rural areas or in run-down sections of the inner city provide exceptionally good opportunities.

An old, prestigious church stands in what has recently become a run-down section of Pittsburgh in the States. This church is heavily endowed. The pastor of this church has a great heart for the poor. He has been able to get this old church, which now has fewer than one hundred people in Sunday morning worship, to commit its vast financial resources to ministry among the poor who live in the immediate vicinity. The church now sponsors a lunch club, a day-care service, a counselling centre, a job-finding service and a legal advice centre. There is a constant flow of people in and out of this church every day. In terms of attendance at worship, the church is still small. In terms of service to the poor, it has never been greater.

A pastor in Kansas City in the States has taken on a similar kind of ministry. In her case, the church is not endowed, and its people can just barely scrape together the money to pay her salary. Nevertheless, she has made sure that the church serves the poor in a variety of ways. Securing funds from the missionary department of her denomination as well as from some other Christian organisations, she has established ministries to old and young alike.

Some people who have been touched by these ministries have begun to attend the church. A wealthy elderly man once asked the pastor why all these 'strange people' were attending the services. She gently answered, 'Because everybody should have the chance to meet Jesus.'

The man responded, 'I suppose you're right. They need Jesus too—'

The pastor interrupted: 'I don't mean them. I mean you!'

Indeed, the pastor was right. By helping the church reach out to the poor, she gave its people the chance to meet Christ face to face. Our Lord always waits to be encountered among the poorest of the poor. In them he bids us to come and love him. Therefore, bringing the middle class and wealthier members of that church into fellowship with the poor will prove to be one of the best ways for the pastor to meet the spiritual hungers of all her parishioners.

44

Finance

Any urban economist knows that one of the primary problems of poor communities is that they have a shortage of banks, or they have banks that do not put a high enough priority on serving their communities. For instance, if the poor put their money in a bank (yes, the poor do put money in banks) that then invests it outside their community, then the community is denied the capital needed to create jobs, improve property and make the personal loans required for buying cars or financing education. But in most poor communities there is usually an absence of any kind of bank at all. Banks find poor communities both unprofitable and dangerous.

In Pittsburgh in the States, a Christian businessman has developed a savings and loan bank that is deliberately set in the African-American community and makes money available to poor families who want to make home improvements or purchase property. In Philadelphia in the States, churches have joined together to start similar savings and loan banks. But even more promising possibilities may exist in the development of credit unions. Some of these have been developed under the auspices of African-American churches. Credit unions are basically banks that lend money to their own members, who, in turn, are the depositors.

Fiscal institutions such as these, which serve the poor, are in desperate need if there are to be means to finance the redevelopment of poor communities in a way that does not

111

displace their present inhabitants. Christians with a heart for the poor who also have the skills to organise and run such institutions must step forward to do this work. The contributions that could be made to poor communities by such servants of Christ are immense.

For further information contact:

Association of British Credit Unions Ltd
Unit 307
Westminster Business Square
339 Kennington Lane
London
SE11 5QY
071–582 2626

The National Federation of Credit Unions
13 Fairfax Crescent
Bierley
Bradford
West Yorkshire
BD4 6BP
(0274) 687692

45

Politics

Those who want to help the poor and have the courage and drive to run for public office can place themselves in positions where they can do a lot of good for a lot of people. Politics often has a bad name among Christians, and there is cynicism about anybody who succeeds in this sometimes dirty profession. But if we took the time really to investigate matters, we would find that most politicians are good public servants who are doing their best to make government work for the people.

Some of the best work for the poor and oppressed can be done at local and national levels of government. Appropriations for public housing, determination of public assistance programmes for the poor, provision of medical programmes for those with low incomes, and supervision of police protection for low-income communities all fall within the spheres of control of politicians on the lower levels of government.

Holding such relatively low-level positions as magistrates or judges cannot be overvalued as far as doing good for the poor is concerned. Settling what some might consider minor claims can be of major concern for those who have little money to spare. Settling car accident cases, determining who gets to keep or lose driver's licences in drunk driving cases, working out whether landlords have been treating tenants fairly—decisions in a host of cases that might seem relatively unimportant in the grand scheme of the judicial system may mean the difference between hope and despair for the poor.

Standing for public office is not as difficult as most outsiders to the political process might assume. Political parties on the ward level are usually looking for candidates who will work hard to be elected. There is a lot of tedious labour that goes with politics (like delivering campaign literature from door to door), but for those who want to make a difference for the poor, careers in politics can prove to be a gratifying means for doing good.

Movement for Christian Democracy
c/o David Alton, MP
House of Commons
London
SW1A 0AA
071–219 3454

Section 4

FURTHER EDUCATION

This book represents just the beginning of the adventure of caring. If God has given you a special love for this world's hungry people, then we'd like to help you go further.

The last five ideas in the book are educational ideas. In them we summarise the sorts of materials out there that are helping thousands of Christians make a difference.

Proverbs 19:2 says, 'It is not good to have zeal without knowledge'. We hope these resources get you well on your way towards informed, compassionate service.

46

Books

Go to your local bookshop to see if it carries these titles. If not, give the bookshop assistant the publisher's name, and he or she will be glad to order the book for you.

Ronald J. Sider, *Rich Christians in an Age of Hunger* (Hodder: London, 1978). The all time classic primer.

Gordon Aeschliman, *Global Trends* (InterVarsity Press: Illinois, USA, 1990).

David Alton, *Faith in Britain: How do Christians Respond to Living in a Materialistic Society?* (Hodder: London, 1991).

Fran Beckett, *Called to Action: Resources and Practical Advice in Helping the Needy* (Fount: London, 1989).

Lester R. Brown, editor, *State of the World: A Worldwatch Institute Report on Progress Toward a Sustainable Society*. Another annual publication, released in the UK by W. W. Norton, London.

Duncan B. Forrester and Danus Skewe, *Just Sharing: A Christian Approach to the Distribution of Wealth, Income and Benefits* (Epworth: London, 1988).

Steve Hayner and Gordon Aeschliman, editors, Global Issues Bible Study Series (InterVarsity Press: Illinois, USA, 1990). A series of twelve booklets, each with an essay on a particular world need followed by six one-hour Bible studies.

Frank Kaleb Jansen, editor, *Target Earth* (Global Mapping Project: California, USA, 1989).

118   FURTHER EDUCATION

John Perkins, *With Justice for All* (Regal Books: California, USA, 1982).

Arthur Simon, *Harvesting Peace: The Arms Race and Human Need* (Sheed & Ward: Missouri, USA, 1990).

Arthur Simon, editor, *State of the Hungry World* (Bread for the World: Washington DC, USA). A new edition is issued each year.

Mike Starkey, *Born to Shop: Consumerism and the Global Dustbin* (Monarch: Tunbridge Wells, 1989).

Paul Valley, *Bad Samaritans: First World Ethics and Third World Debt* (Hodder: London, 1991).

47

Videos

These videos focus on the needs of people primarily in urban areas. They make for good education for understanding the poor because the city centre is where tomorrow's poor will live.

Somebody Up There Loves Me. Testimonies from inner city Christians in Liverpool. Available from: Sunrise Video Productions, 13 King Edward Avenue, Worthing, West Sussex BN14 8DB, telephone (0903) 205583.

Hope for the City. Shows how Christians in Amsterdam and other cities have responded to the challenge of urban mission. Available from: Youth With A Mission, 13 Highfield Oval, Ambrose Lane, Harpenden, Hertfordshire AL5 4BX, telephone (0582) 765481.

Good Neighbours. Two case studies from Wolverhampton and Preston on engaging in mission in Asian communities. Available from: BCMS Crosslinks, 251 Lewisham Way, London SE4 1XF, telephone 081–691 6111.

Does Anyone Care? Shows the work that is being done under the Churches Urban Fund by urban priority area churches. Available from: Archbishop's Officer for Urban Priority Areas, Church House, Great Smith Street, London SW1P 3NZ, telephone 071–222 7011.

Can Do. Stories of urban Christians in Leeds and London. Available from: Archbishop's Officer for Urban Priority Areas (address above).

Broken Image. Looking at urban life in the third world country of the Philippines, filmed in Manila and Surigao city, and the implications

119

of the good news for the poor. Featuring Garth Hewitt, Stewart Henderson and J. Geoffrey Stevenson. Available from: Tear Fund, 100 Church Road, Teddington, Middlesex TW11 8QE, telephone 081–977 9144.

48

Specialist Organisations

Three organisations who are specially focused to help you in your commitment to the hungry. It is well worth becoming a supporter of Tear Fund and regularly receiving their quarterly magazine, *Tear Times*, so that you can stay current on the issues related to hunger, and find out about other resources. The Evangelical Coalition for Urban Mission (ECUM) provides resources and networking for Christians who want to relocate to areas of poverty. It is also well worth writing to World Vision of Britain.

ECUM
(Evangelical Coalition for Urban Mission)
85a Allerton Road
Liverpool
Merseyside
L18 2DA
051–722 8145

World Vision of Britain
Dychurch House
8 Abington Street
NN1 2AJ
(0604) 22964

Tear Fund
100 Church Road
Teddington
Middlesex
TW11 8QE
081–977 9144

49

Magazines

Worldwatch is a bi-monthly that keeps you current on global issues ranging from environment to poverty. In the States, the annual subscription cost is $15. You would need to write to them for details on how to subscribe in Great Britain.

Worldwatch
1776 Massachusetts Avenue NW
Washington, DC 20036
USA

World Development is a free, high quality journal published by the United Nations Development Programme.

World Development Journal
UN Development Programme
One UN Plaza
New York, NY 10017
USA

Together is a quarterly published by World Vision International. Its focus is community development. It is available in the UK from:

MARC Europe
Vision Building
4 Footscray Road
Eltham
London
SE9 2TZ
081–294 1989

Also recommended are:

The Monthly Bulletin
OXFAM
274 Banbury Road
Oxford
OX2 7DZ
(0865) 311311

SPUR
World Development Movement
25 Beehive Place
London
SW9 7QR
071–737 6215

50

Mailing Lists

Many relief and development organisations would love to receive your donations to assist them in their efforts. They produce magazines and newsletters that keep their donors up to date. Write to them and ask to be put on their regular mailing list. If in time you decide to give, that's your choice, but meanwhile you can benefit from their insights and information.

Tear Fund
100 Church Road
Teddington
Middlesex
TW11 8QE
081–977 9144

OXFAM
274 Banbury Road
Oxford
OX2 7DZ
(0865) 311311

Christian Aid
PO Box 100
London
SE1 7RT
071–620 4444

World Vision of Britain
Dychurch House
8 Abington Street
NN1 2AJ
(0604) 22964